THIS IS I

Enrico Suave

ISBN: 978-976-97031-2-4

Editing / Book Layout by

Passionate Words
Editing Services

(IG @passionate.words.editing246)

ACKNOWLEDGMENTS

I would like to thank God for the ability to write these experiences of my life and thoughts in poetic form.

God, thank you for the courage to share my life through this book and for never losing faith in me, even when I lost faith in myself. Thanks to Dads (my late Grandfather) who was the greatest man to ever walk this earth in my lifetime and without whose unconditional love, along with his teachings, I would not be half the man I am today, for which I am eternally grateful. I want to thank my Queen, Greta St. Hill. The sacrifices you have made for me have become the pillar of my success and I appreciate you for being with me through all the changing scenes of my life. Thank you to my family, friends, and supporters for motivating and believing in me every step of my journey. A very special mention to my friends and colleagues, Kendra Wilkinson, Leah Newton, Lucy Wilson, Deiranda Alleyne, Kevon Edey, Keoma Mallet, Ramone Blackman, Irijah Tha Don, Asantie Murrell and Nylah Wilkinson for your inspiration, guidance, honest reviews, and critiques.

Thanks to my co-poets La Shawna Griffith, Janine Garnett and Dante Alexi for assisting on the project and bringing my story to life.

Last, but certainly not least, I want to thank Jamie Davis for taking the official photograph which was used for the cover of this book and Akeem Chandler-Prescod for the artwork on the cover. Finally thank you to Onika Newsam-Proverbs, you have been nothing short of motivational, supportive and an ever-present part of my journey and I would not have been able to do this book without you in my corner.
I appreciate you all.
Thank you.

Enrico.

Table of Contents

Dedication

DADS

I know you are in a better place
But I would give the world to see your face,
To see you smile, to see you laugh,
To hear your voice, to share your space.
To have conversations about the past
As you passed life lessons onto me along the way.
To this day I still dream of you,
Teaching me how to play the piano.
Showing me how to change a light switch,
And explaining all that you used to do.
I think about the time when I was going away,
You took time to be by my side and, in that way,
You were saying you were here to stay.
So when I look to the skies I see you through the rays,
I remember the kite flying days that we shared,
Random drives in G299 are treasures I hold dear.
Supermarket runs, picking up anything I wished –
Now all I wish is for one last moment to tell you this:
I miss how you were towards everyone you met,
Day ones or recent acquaintances – you were a joy to all of
them.
But your greatest joy was entertaining your grandchildren,
With your jokes, your gaffs and just purely being Dads.
I have mentioned the good times of which they were many,
And when the bad times came, your light still shone brightly,
A true warrior to the end, my grandfather, my friend,
It was never goodbye, but simply, I will see you again.

Family

THIS IS I

ROSES

Just like the roses from your valentine mean the world to
you,
So do these roses in mine.
Fortunate just to have them, and I give my word to you,
A woman's work is worth more than just time.

My Queen?
She was grinding to provide me with a better life.
It was cold times but her mindset gave me the drive
To look in anyone's eyes and say,
"I'll be a success!"
She watched her son rise and saw her son set.

To my Grannies and aunties, I love you dearly,
I know I was once that problem child like Junior in the 90's.
But I will always hold on to everything you taught me,
Because your lessons are the blessings that make me, me.

To my loving JuJu and others like you,
You weren't there from inception but I still have mad af-
fection for you.
I may not express it often but know I mean what I say,
I appreciate you in every single way, on a daily basis.

To persons who are still learning how to make mistakes,
Uncle Vito remembers the promise that he made, and to
this day

I will protect you with my life because you are my heart,
And the joy you bring to me no-one can take apart.
If the world was to end right now,
I'll ensure you're one of the 144, 000 that makes it to
God.

Last but not least, to my boss ladies,
You've seen me cry, you've seen me fly; through it all
you stood by me.
You are the best friends that anyone can have
And if I pass, may these words be with you for eternity.

THIS IS MY HOME

Golden sands touched by crystal blue waters,
Shape a country united by its pride,
Built upon an industry that stretches 166 sq. miles.

This is my home Barbados,
My island in the sun;
Finally independently independent,
A strong Republica.

A diamond in the rough, this is who we are,
Now forging forward as craftsmen of our own craftsman-
ship,
Great expectations we will exceed,
In strength and unity.

Our journey may be heavy,
Yet 287, 000 hands make light work.
The higher we rise, greater will our nation grow,
Whether near or far, no matter where we roam – d
Barbados,
This is my home.

DYING TO SURVIVE

The audacity that we have, to step out into their light,
Like – who do we really think we are?
When they see us, you know they'll want to fight,
But the truth is, we are used to these scars.

It's been a long time coming, yet we are still far,
Four hundred plus years later,
Our ancestors fought the fights that we are fighting but
still…
No justice, no peace, no favours.

Guns drawn on us just because we are black,
Then they will turn and say 'all lives matter'.
No they don't! Who are you really feeding those lies to?
'Cause all I'm seeing is racial attack.

But our colour is what scares you?
Fine!
Take it away!
Take your colour away too and see that we are the
same.
The only difference is that you were not – no –
You are not enslaved,
So you do not feel our daily pain.

We are tired of being oppressed,

Depressed in this mindset that you have continuously
made us digest.
Knees on our necks for false checks and less
While you, the majority, have your peaceful rests.
Children being asked, "What do you want to be when
you grow up?"
Their answer is "Alive!"
So tell me, when will we as a people show up?
Because right now, we are dying to survive.

This poem is dedicated to:
George Floyd, Ahmaud Arbery,
Tamir Rice, Sandra Bland,
Eric Garner, Trayvon Martin
and many, many, many others!

BERTA, BERTA

Are we strong?
Strong enough to break free from these chains?
Take the whips from their hands, hand them the same
fate that our forefathers faced?
Are we strong?
Strong enough to rewrite the wrongs?
Sing the songs that cotton fields were blessed with in
times where our rights were wronged?

Tell me,
Are we?
Are we strong enough to walk the mental underground
railroads?
To escape the mental bondage that we have unfortu-
nately been bestowed?
Are we strong?
Strong enough to endure the tears from our ancestors'
cheeks?
Worn when they were weak by the mills every week?

Still, I speak, still, I seek,
Still, I am asking because the pain cuts deep!
Blue is the sea that carries the buried souls we breathe
So will we reap what we sowed and ascend to our
peak?

Tell me, can we tweak the narrative?

Speak the relative things that make us unique?
Like our relatives expressing who we are through an-
tiques.
Can we please just practice what we preach?

Will we face everything and rise?
Or
Forget everything and run?
That's two types of fear, but I hope we choose the right
one.
Daughters and sons, loved ones and those gone,
Will we be strong or will we let them carry on?

Taking us on a trip we were never supposed to be on,
To foreign lands when the motherland is our home.
So let me know if we are ready to fight the plight of the
struggle,
And rise up like a Phoenix from the ashes and the rubble.

LOVING SERENITY

There are volumes spoken of the agony of female realities

After being silenced by fear from years of their mental brutality.

Tears streaming down their faces from disgraceful male species,

To experience a high while making them feel low, it is a travesty.

Honestly, it is a tragedy to see Serenity contemplating suicide,

An inkling she had from the filth she felt inside due to his senseless pride.

He was happy taking her for a ride; she was lying there wanting to die,

Her NO's being denied as he nose-dived between her thighs.

He looked into her flooded eyes and, with no sympathy,
He simply continued until he was fully empty.

She lay there unable to explain this now-etched memory,
An unwarranted chemistry with his body.

That chemistry that robs the body of its natural biology,
But yet, through physics, transforms the energy transferred into screams of agony.

Down to the very vibrations of the atmosphere, pain resonates and floods the air.

Time ceased; she stood still, but yet he got up and left her bare.

But beware, Serenity was one of many.
"Manly men" un-bending the strength of these ladies,
And it kills me to know that they wear fear on their
sleeves,
Wearing mascara to mask what they received,
Eye shadow to shadow the blows that showed their cry-
ing pleas,
Silenced when all they wanted to do was speak.
These are some of the reasons why women hate men. I
mean, why they would not?
We cherish them for a second and by the hour we view
them as thots.
We see them as objects, subjecting them to a class that
they are not,
Subtracting their value, adding fear, multiplying their
pain, and dividing their thoughts…
That equals to naught!
If you ask me, these types of men are the real bitches!
No purposeful bark, only looking for women to scratch
their itches.
You men are rags undeserving of their riches,
Leaving scars where there were beauty marks, you
frauds deserve stitches.
Women are independent, yes –
But aren't we supposed to protect them?
Love them beyond the figment of their imagination?
Be their safe haven in this world of corruption?
Be the piece that perfectly fits in their puzzle?
Be their peace in their struggle?
Be their rock when their foundation is unstable?

But, most of all, cherish them completely when they're
unable?
Yet, who we think are men are just little boys wanting to
hustle.
Trying to see how many females they could juggle;
No respect for the opposite gender, just putting a label
on saying "return to sender,"
And here you are taking her for granted what she has
surrendered.
Her love, trust, and beauty in all of her splendour.

AN ODE TO A FLOWER

Dear women,
You deserve a love that doesn't require you suffering first.
You deserve someone that values your daily worth.
You deserve someone that understands that your body
and mind are a temple,
Someone who doesn't complicate your life, but keeps it
simple.
You deserve someone who is interested in what you're
into,
Someone who takes time to appreciate the beauty of
you.
You are a masterpiece in God's gallery,
You are the essence that makes our presence one of so-
lidity.
You are the atmosphere, by which our sphere is in taking,
You are breathtaking. Smile! It's captivating.
You deserve love in the finest sense,
You deserve someone who does more than just say it.
You deserve sex that matters,
Because recreational sex is no longer it.
You deserve quality time with a quality guy
Who brings you peace of mind and that's it.
So dear women, hopefully you find that guy that fits the
bill,
Who treats you as you are supposed to and caters to you
at will.

Who sees you for everything that I mentioned and under-
stands truly
That you are a phenomenal woman who is to be loved
phenomenally.
23

THE BEAUTY OF AFFECTION

Where did women get this notion that guys don't require
affection?
I'm asking because we as men don't receive it as much
as we give.
Now I'm not saying that all women don't show it and that
all men require it,
But here is some advice to those that neglected to ac-
knowledge it.
Women, we too like to be held,
We too like to be complimented.
We too like to feel appreciated
And feel like it's reciprocated.
We like to know that we are your men in public as well as
in private.
Instead of being skimmed, portrayed as a friend;
We want to be told those sweet nothings as well,
And wake up to texts we didn't expect you to send.
When we see you ladies, our eyes open wide.
The sight of you is enough to turn our frowns to smiles.
When you speak, our ears listen attentively to the beauty
of your voice,
Our hearts express gratitude to us for making the right
choice.
When we hug you,
Do you feel that emotion?
That sense that we've been missing you, wanting your
devotion?

When you see us,
What goes through your minds?
Is it the same feeling that we feel every time we share
time?
No pretending, we want to know you mean it all,
Not just a show that closes at the curtain call.
Not just an infatuation to provide us with temporary satis-
faction,
But sustainable energy that consists of reciprocation.
I guess there's this misconception that we are always to
be tough,
That we are callous by nature, emotionless and rough.
We are not that way though, if I am being real,
We just need that person that knows the deal.
See us with the hard shell but the soft detail inside,
See us as equals and not just by your side.
We are your men and we carry that with pride,
So just let us know if you are down for the ride.

Conflicting

E.M.O.T.I.O.N.S.

T
H
I
S

I
S

I

E.M.O.T.I.O.N.S

Do we people ever ask the question: what are emotions?

I think emotions are…
Every Mood Or Thoughtful Intuition On Natural Sensations.

The origin of these sensations can come from human action or nature's bliss,
Such as a beautiful rainbow in the sky,
Or that one majestic unforgettable kiss.

That amazing feeling can easily switch up into a dreadful,
Distasteful and unforgiving curse,
It is well known that emotions bring out our best reactions, and our worst.
But let us stop for a second and break it down a little bit more,
Please stay tuned as we enter the poetic shuttle to go and explore.

You see love and happiness?
Those two can hold hands forever,
They are the major contributors to one's futuristic endeavours.
Real love has the power to awaken the heart, soul and mind,
And true happiness presents itself out of nowhere
And prepares it to last for a lifetime.

The complete opposite to those are hatred and sadness.
Sometimes we ask ourselves, what causes us to express
emotions of such agony and malice?
Hatred is mainly fueled by hostility, jealousy and disgust,
While sadness expresses pain and disappointment,
maybe in someone who you thought you could trust.

Trust takes patience and can be considered a coura-
geous act,
Also admiration of one's character can give them the
confidence in which they might lack.
The quote "Fortune favours the brave" probably illustrates
confidence and courage the best,
Such influential words can easily put you a couple steps
ahead of the rest.

But to sum it up,
Life is a cycle of various emotional contents,
Ranging from a small shred of guilt to a substantial
amount of embarrassment.
What we choose to feel in the end will always be our
choice,
The key to understanding your emotions is by listening to
each one's distinct and unique voice.

BROKEN

Staring in the broken mirror,
Broken pieces of myself, shattered.
Broken promises from your lips I gathered.
Looking at each one, wondering if it matters.

Said you would fix my broken heart
But left it unguarded.
Said you won't do what she did
But look – you overdid it.

You had me with your words, you lost me with your ac-
tions,
I kept going back hoping for a new reaction.
A different feel, but from you it's unrequited affection,
Now I'm standing with grenades in hand as it is a fatal at-
traction.

ALADDIN

I wish that I can be the reason that you're online most of
the time,
Especially late at night before the sandman fills your
eyes.
Others get your speeches leaving me speechless and, in
my mind,
You are downplaying what is really an upward climb for
me.

And I am watching you bypass me every second of ev-
ery minute,
Like a genie in a bottle waiting to escape from it
Trapped in your magic lamp hoping it doesn't break or
disintegrate,
Expecting you to sooner or later hand me my fate.

I wish that I didn't feel this painful subject of heartache,
Cause my heart ached for you now my heart aches
bruised because of you.
Brewed like beer, I was bared for you,
Emptied until I was see through.
Scared to show my scars sacred only for your views,
In the memory of your window sill still I wish to be your
view.

Still I wish the cents in my money till made sense to add
up,

Because it's costing me everything just to show you my
love.
Filling cannons to imprint the iron ship in which you sail,
So you can understand the depths of how I feel.

Realize that I'm thinking about the long run going down
the Elaine,
And it isn't just to give you my D but so you can see how I
can be when I'm on my A game.
This isn't checkers, you are the queen that lays on my
chest.
It's your move.
Am I a pawn that you can step on any chance you get?
Nah! On nights you saw this knight waiting to the dawn
for you, less you forget.
A rook that went to the bishop just so he can be a true
King for you,
A vow to protect.

Now I'm just a Quasimodo in your Notre Dame,
Better yet, I'm Aladdin without his Jasmine.
Like a lost scented fragrance in my garden, disheart-
ened,
A lost picture to my imperfect frame.

DETACHED

When was the last time you said "I love you" first?
When was the last time you kissed me just because you
could?
When was the last time you looked me in my eyes all
happy?
When was the last time you didn't experience those
things with me?

When was the last time you had butterflies in your stom-
ach?
Excited to see me, nervous when around me feeling in
your gut?
When was the last time you watched me sleep peace-
fully?
When was the last time you didn't experience those
things with me?

When was the last time you told me, "You're glad to be
mine?"
When was the last time you accepted me telling you,
"Gosh damn you're so fine?"
When was the last time you called my phone just to hear
me?
Tell me when was the last time you didn't experience
those things with me?

So many questions consume my mind,

To the point where I feel left behind inside
The confined space that is you and I
With no place to run, and nowhere to hide.

So I come to you just wondering why?
Why do I feel like others are special to you while
I look to experience experiences with my Ms. Bonnie
Parker,
Only to be seen as the guy from The Parkers.

It gets darker, there's no light where I came from,
You know that extra mile I often take just to show you
you're the one?
Thinking you'll meet me halfway some day,
But you don't, so should I just be on my way?

I wish for this to be the last time I'm expressing myself in
this manner,
We shifted the paradigm but entered an eternal disaster.
So let me know if to go, or if to stay a while,
Cause I'm tired of being the only one going the extra
mile.

TRAPPED

These are not just words but a deep burden,
Trapped in a closet, unable to let go
From the hurt that you caused when you promised that
you won't,
But I will no longer be comforted from your promises any-
more.

Hearing the words "I love you"
Only for you to purposely do what you did.
To satisfy what?!
I don't know, but you lost your best friend instead.

Like seriously who does that to the person they claim is
their everything?
The person who's been there for you through thick and
thin?!
Who would lose to make sure you win?!
Now that's interesting...

Funny thing is you think I'm supposed to just get over it,
You sleeping with another person while I was too busy
being in love with you to see it.
Trying to start anew with you despite the pain,
Why didn't I leave when you cheated again?

I think it's because we shared something so real
And I was so into you I didn't know exactly how to feel.

Didn't know one day you would stab me in the back
I never knew love could hurt this fucking bad.

Now I'm so sick of every damn love song I hear,
Never been here before and I wish now to disappear.
Because the perfectly imperfect girl I thought I knew
Has me perfectly screwed and there's nothing I can do.

FAITHFUL LIES

Don't introduce me to a vibe that you know
You aren't going to maintain.
Don't invite me in then have me feeling like I'm the one
that's going insane,
Thinking it's love on the brain,
Pain seen through the tears that I have rained for you.
And no umbrella can shelter me from what you have put
me through,
Threw my heart your way only for you to do what you
said you wouldn't do.

I saw behind your eyes, never expected you to be rob in
disguise,
I thought you were the Robin in the skies that flew in my
mind, but it was just lies.
So why owe you this pensive pen work when it would
sieve through?
It's so my cursive blade's ink can sink deep within you,
like I was deep within you.

I'm not talking deep within your pink,
I'm talking deep within you to think!
Don't you remember when our minds once upon a time
were in sync?
Now you're gone on your solo mission, but what goes
around comes around,

That's why I didn't cry you a river; instead, I looked in the
mirror, and found all that I have lost.

It's that I'm worth an unearthed vibe birthed within the
dirt that will grow over time,
Not to over shine nor undermine but exude peace of
mind when I'm with mine.
But until that time I will be fine,
I hope your grass is greener on the other side,
After all, I guess I was just a guest of your faithful lies.

EMPTY

Not fueled enough with emotions,
No charge left in my battery,
This emptiness inside of me
Brought out another side of me.

See I'm watching for the time,
That you might pass me by,
Every second looking at the minutes,
Where our love was well defined.

Memorabilia of you and I
Was etched in my mind at one point in time,
'Til that breaking point when we broke,
Now that point is killing us inside.

Side by side we used to ride along,
Now my heart is cold like ice.
Put those cubes in my liquor...
Toast to this wretched life.

WINDOW PAIN

Sitting by the windowpane,
Thinking of the pain you caused,
Wishing upon the night stars,
That the memories of you are lost
Into the abyss, where I felt your last kiss,
Where I felt your last touch,
Where I often wonder if
We could go back to when we were on track,
Running through this maze together,
Side by side we attacked
Every obstacle head on,
Now it seems like we're both gone,
Into different directions,
And I'm thinking, "How did this happen?"
But the love is too far gone.
So I reminisce daily and I gain
Myself again so I'll refrain
From thinking negative thoughts,
And hope positivity reigns
While I'm sitting by the windowpane.

P.O.V.

He sees the world as his playground,
He listens to its hollow sound.
His life taking beatings, pound for pound.
He seeks to make a rebound.

He tried to give up his heart,
But she played a vital part,
In him departing, distorted.
His world of light is now dark.

He is his own alibi,
Hiding the truth behind his eyes.
He seeks answers from the night sky.
He, my friend...is I.

PLAYBOY

Fuck love and all that mushy shit,
Clearly it means nothing, so what's the point of it?
Bring the cookie, let me treat it, eat it, please it and get it
over with...
And other than that, get to stepping.

Cause I gave my all to one woman,
And that one woman dissed me.
That one woman looked me dead in my eyes
And said,
"Hey!
Goodbye!
Don't miss me!"
Seriously?!

After all we've been through?
After all we've shared?
After she had no one,
Am I the only one that cared?

Damn!
I never imagined,
I never feared this day
In my mind we were growing, now she's going away.
Saying it was just a season and there's a reason, but
fuck's sake,

What happened to being in love? Now all I'm feeling is
hate.

But look, I'm still fighting like a soldier –
Suave don't even do it, don't turn into that old person.
While she's over there entertaining fuckboys...
Looking on, sometimes I wish I was still a playboy.

UNTIL

I have been caging my thoughts just to appease you,
Just to make sure that you are assured.
But behind the closed doors of my mind, I am fearful
That I am killing myself to be yours.

Because without realizing I was internally bleeding,
I was a friend to my being without a potion for healing.
I was at a crossroads, opposing those that tried to show
That there is more for my life and I need to let go.

But I can't!
Instead, I continue to cause self-inflicted wounds
Because I have hurt the person I valued most with actions I cannot undo.
And since then though I have changed, deep in your mental is the before,
So, I will climb up a mountain to get to the place where we will be restored.
Rest assured that I will make it to the top 'cause you are my peak and more,
But until that moment comes just know that this is from the core.

LOVE & RESPECT

Where do love and respect come from?
Without them, besides death what would be life's natural outcome?
They say that respect isn't given but it is earned,
But before you get it, how much of your soul do you have to burn?
Love is a feeling which is amazing when expressed by most, if not all,
But when things go bad, where is that special someone to catch you when you fall?
I always believe that to know is the hardest part,
You then protect yourself by putting an ice box over your broken heart.
Being treated like garbage is something that no one in this world deserves,
Whether with a physical gesture or with terrible words.
Allow yourself to be free in a cruel world such as this,
At some point, everyone will have to take a swing and miss.
No matter the situation, always stay positive,
Sometimes the best things in life will decide to take the initiative.
For now, fight through the pain and ignore the fake friends and conditional lovers,
Because the love and respect which you once sought will be desired by others.

HER MISTAKES

I'm one broken heart closer
From my heart being stolen,
From the one that God has chosen,
From the one who's heart is outspoken.

Her mistakes left me awakened,
So no more will I be taken
By the dungeon of her false love
And her lying affection.

For I cared painfully,
The pain fully expressed by her iniquities.
Drained from her unsustainable energy
And the memories?
Well, they're history.

Now I'm intended to find the one that completes,
Not the one that makes me compete.
Not one that causes distance
But rather takes this stance with me.

To have and to hold in unison
Where we are universally recognized as one.
Where we embody no toxicity,
We simply embody each other's love.

This was not easy to say,

Just like I know for the right woman it may be hard to
take.
But I'm a man with a plan, who understands what is at
stake,
A man who won't let you pay for her mistakes.

Love:
REBIRTH

THIS IS I

BASICS

What is really necessary when it comes to being in a
relationship?
Is one well aware of the importance of entering this
emotional partnership?
So much has to be taken into consideration if you're go-
ing to do something like this,
As every predicament encountered can't be rectified
with just a simple kiss.
We tend to make a relationship out to be a need rather
than a want,
Forgetting to check off all the boxes and commence it
with a premature launch.
Whatever happened to building a powerful connection
without physical pleasure?
Of course I mean sex, is that the consolation prize
awarded while one ignores the real treasure?
The feelings of a human being are so delicate and easily
manipulated,
For example, being lied to and underappreciated
When you really thought that person was honest and
dedicated.
Terrible things like that certainly aren't expected out of
such a precious commitment,
One expects to be shown compassion and loyalty or
what we Bajans call 'De Propa Treatment'.
It is better to get to know that person more and just have
spontaneous fun,

Things will become clearer, while the attraction elevates to a significantly higher level in the long run.
Most of all, develop a friendship so robust it is unbreak-able,
Embrace each moment with your heart and suddenly you start to imagine the unthinkable,
Although you're taking it slow, time is very precious, so be sure not to waste it,
There is no reason to complicate things. You want my advice? I'd say...just stick to the basics.

NEVER FADES AWAY

The love which we seek is not so easily found,
So untraceable it passes by us at the speed of sound,
But when we do find it, what do we do next?
Do we try our best to nurture it?
Or do we get rid of it like it's an unwanted text?
It doesn't sound like the wisest thing to do,
One would be very miserable,
Just like all humans in life, we all just want to be happy
and comfortable,
But, as usual, it is taken for granted by most people who
are not ready.
They believe that a relationship is always going to be
easy, strong and steady.
Well, most of the time that is how it starts,
If not respected or taken care of,
Right before your eyes it could all simply fall apart.
I bet that is the last thing that anyone would like to hap-
pen,
It can be so painful and so cruel,
Even one's sadness would be saddened,
It's best to hold on and develop it into something special.
Once you believe in love, you will then be introduced to
its true potential,
But just remember to take it step by step and day by day,
Because it is the kind of feeling you would want to never
fade away.

MY LIGHTHOUSE

As my eyes look to the sea's blue
There I see you, a ray kissing the shore,
And I am sure that you are heaven sent,
An earth angel in your element, a blessing to my soul.

Your beauty is so unique that I gained a speech impedi-
ment,
Lost in my attraction, your traction pulls me in.
A whim to be in your binocular depth perception,
From inception 'til our life's ending.

I know our love story is pending,
If I could just muster the courage to get up and walk to
you,
To express my thoughts while we embed footprints in the
sand,
To create something new, something true with you.

So, on this day that is sunny like Liston,
With the horizon as wide as the smile that you're wearing
And your hair moving like the water just flowing.
There is just one thing I'd like to ask you:
Will you be mine?

LOVE JONES

Say Nina, can I be your man for all seasons?
I know it's hard to feel love when your heart experienced
treason
But my interest from the first night when we took flight is
the reason
Why I think you're worth the time, effort and this procla-
mation.

A new sensation that's so refreshing, something I've not
been expecting,
Something that life didn't grant me, but now I see it was
timing.
God was simply mapping the path out to lead me right
to you
Now I know every lyric of my heart was written intention-
ally for you.

So step to my scene,
I'll introduce you to a vibe you've never seen,
Where every moment is a memoir etched in our history.
Where the smile upon on your face is as wide as a field of
daisies,
I could look at it all day while we're in the bed being lazy.

You are a beauty mark in this world
But in my world, you are Oshun.
And it may be too soon to say,

So, in time, I hope that you're swooned.
For the joy that's deep within me is a product of what
you exude,
A new tune I sing because of you – rhythm and blues.

So as the double bass plays in the background, Nina you are
Every star in my galaxy,
Every beat of my heart.
Simply put in the words of H.E.R and Daniel Caesar
If life is a movie, then you're the best part.

YOUR HEART'S ATTIRE

Can I undress your heart?
Remove the satin dress that you're wearing and expose
your scars?
The scars that aren't really scars
Just abstract art that depicts your masterpiece.

Pieced together imperfectly,
Perfectly hiding the true beauty that lies underneath,
'Cause you were lied to from men of deceit
But now that the seat is vacant, can I be what you
need?

Can I shower you with love that you've never received?
Be your towel to cover every intricate detail of your be-
ing?
As my arms open to your grace and silky feeling.
May these things be the reason that you're healing.

As I am mesmerized by the touch of your bubbly effer-
vescence
Covered up with the smell of your enchanting presence.
In essence, your essence is pure
And I wish to pour my unfailing love into your fountain, of
this, I'm sure.

So can I re-dress your heart?
Place a silk dress on your body that still exposes your

beauty marks?
The beauty marks that are the arts on your masterpiece.
Pieced together imperfectly,
Perfectly showing the true beauty that lies underneath.

DOUX ET EPICE

I'm trying to have my bed scented with your fragrance,
While having conversations about our future together.
Kissing you in between sentences
Just because I find your lips to look and taste amazing,
Have you losing your thoughts like, "What was I saying?"

Then I'll glide my fingers along every inch of your being,
Until they slide into your slippery pride
Causing your body language to start speaking.
Expletives you express vocally complimenting your moan-
ing,
As my tongue traces where the fingers went scoping.

See my intentions are to explore every element of you,
And appreciate you in ways that no man ever could do.
Love you for who you are
And everything that you're not,
Like how you loved me for who I was when I started at
naught.

So I proceed to infuse your essence with my endowment,
Investing in this moment granted to us with precision.
See this is not a trial;
I'm looking to balance all of the equations,
So we can profit and I can provide you with income.

Shower you with blessings that you have never thought
of,
Go on trips to places that we have never heard of.
But for now, you're in my bed scenting it with your fra-
grance,
And we're having conversations about our future to-
gether.

SIMPLICITY & PERFECTION

Your style and grace make people jealous of me for
knowing you.
The way you look into my eyes
Makes me feel relieved and brand new.
It's almost impossible to separate your personality
From your physical appearance,
They complement each other so well;
It is like an irresistible substance.
You are so beautiful;
You blur the distinction between fiction and reality.
The thing is, for you,
Looking the way you do is an everyday normality.
Dreams can't compare to your alluring smile and voice,
If that was the case,
I would sleep forever without even rethinking my choice.
Sometimes I think about your beautiful lips and damn,
I would love to get a taste.
Feeling the warmth of your gorgeous body
While I wrap my arms around your waist,
As I embrace your touch with my heart's love and pas-
sion combined,
The pureness of your soul overflows in me
Just in time to save mine.
In the words of Wale,
Some people would sell their soul just to buy some atten-
tion,

But you, you don't need to do that
Because you are the true example of simplicity and per-
fection.

61

PROTECTION

Baby, this isn't a poem but a declaration,
A deep devotion of my love for you,
An expression of how you changed my vision so listen
To the things that I would do for you.

I would fight for you
Take the bullets, the blows, the pain,
Crawl over broken glass, stand in the flames,
Push you from in front of a moving train and
Catch all grenades that may go your way.

Safe to say, I'm grateful for what we've got,
So I put myself on the line, making all the shots,
To give you everything because you gave me everything
every other girl has not,
So, I stop in admiration, then proceed with the plot.

Different scenes from this movie that transpires the real
story,
Into the making up of our history and this passionate
chemistry,
Telling every man not to try because you are my mystery,
my Daphne.

A comet in my eyes 'cause I've been waiting all my life
for this moment to see

Your naked soul and baby, it's amazing to be
Feeling your heartbeat from the inside;
Rhythmic emotions like a drum line.

Facing everything and rising,
No fear will consume my mind,
For even when it is not day,
It cannot always be night.

But I vouch to be your knight,
I vouch to be your safe haven.
To be the peace of your puzzle
That you've been missing.

NO MATTER WHAT

When I love you,
It's with my body soul and mind.
I put your happiness before mine,
Actually, your happiness is mine.
See?
When I love you,
I don't care about what consequences come,
It's you that's by my side,
It's you that owns my love.
For when I love you,
You'll see the happy tears in my eyes,
'Cause a real man cries
When he knows where his love lies.
Baby?
When I love you,
Every word comes with an action.
I'm drawn to your passion
And yes, you are my devotion.
So when I say I love you,
I mean that with everything I've got,
And I love that you love me,
And this proves my love won't ever stop.

EPIPHANY

With you, my world is just limitless.
Your spell entraps my heart to confine
The reason for that is effortless:
You are the little light of mine.

So I will let your shine radiate
As the night sky embraces its daily comet
A perfect description of my every wish
Recognition to God, for you are worth it.

You are the articulation of my heart's speech,
Every word absolute and every girl obsolete.
Meekly giving you every facet of my being
You give this man's definition a new meaning.

You're major to what I'm about
This is why I love you –
This is why the Clyde in me comes out,
Because I see the Bonnie in you.

Dangerously devoted to the potency of your mind
As you capture the essence of my presence in Flash time
The positive energy of our electricity intertwined
Setting the stage as we travel through space and time.

Take a step back…now read it backwards.

THE VOW

The journey we have had that led to this moment
Is one that I will not regret.
Memorable threads of highs and lows
Are treasures that cannot be spent.

You have peeled back layers of me
The world has never been privileged to see.
I am reserved out there, yes, but in our atmosphere
I will continue to give you all of me.

Because I never dreamed that this would be my next
chapter,
Finding a soul so pure even when the world was so cold.
Where love was conquered despite life's recent disasters,
Yet, somehow, when I look into your eyes, I see my home.

So as I stand here before you, teary eyed,
Ready to experience life's journeys facing triumphs and
fights,
I'd have it no other way than with you by my side,
Intentionally how it was designed.

Inspiration

THIS IS I

CHAINS

Recently, it has been so difficult to just move forward,
I've been hiding away from my endless thoughts like a
helpless little coward.
Not too sure if I am ready to step into the next chapter of
my life,
Because I'm so afraid it will be like this one, which unfortu-
nately has been full of strife.
Every idea that I shared or commitment made to me was
dismissed or neglected,
Not going to lie, all I really ever wanted was to be ac-
cepted.
Why risk it all when all I feel is nothing but pain and uncer-
tainty?
I would truly hate to fail again because that would just
be a waste of tears and energy.
As usual, it's my negative side that is holding me back,
This side of me has the ability to make me feel useless
and trapped.
Continuously stuck in the bad graces of my enemies and
my demons,
Showered with injustices and displeasing comments for
absolutely no reason.
I want to know, can this be stopped just for the sake of
my peace of mind?
I'd rather live a non-threatening lifestyle and just put this
all behind.

Is there some way to get out of this prison of imaginary
gains?
Or is it possible to become independent and break away
from these chains?

MOMENT OF TRUTH

They say I have changed a lot, but I say a lot has
changed me,
That's why I changed the locks and discarded the old
keys.
It was time to change the plot due to unforeseen scenes
In this movie of my life, even things not seen on the
screen.

For it seemed like my life had been ripped at the seams
On the jeans of my genes passed down to me like a
scheme
See many a person deemed me to never be enough in
their eyes,
Thought to be subpar to my father, even my mother at
times.

Nights of suicide on my mind was the easiest form to
hide,
To Jekyll my way out of this life caused by my inadequa-
cies
See, death was trying to hold me down and I was giving
up to the fiends.
I was a constant mistake filled with failed opportunities.

Yet, within this Garden of Eden, I rose,
To let my former self go because my past is closed.
My present is a gift and my future is untold,

Don't be sold by my words, but by the actions of my soul
That floats in life's river, delivered through my ebb and
flows.

So, to those that wish to change their locks and discard
the old keys,
To those that wish to change their plots due to unfore-
seen scenes,
Grasp every opportunity before it's too late,
Let the dash between your two dates equate to some-
thing great.

REFLECTIONS

As my mind recollects on opportunities missed,
I reminisce on the fact that I was the one that failed my-
self.
Blame passed onto others in an effort to save face,
But in reality, it was my mindset that caused my fate.

Even when I had and still have others looking up to me,
Behind my smile is a feeling of inferiority and insecurity.
While I project positivity and encouraging words to those
around,
My sound is in surround by the thoughts of my hollow
ground.

But if I am to manifest greatness, I must first digest
My past for what it was and let my present project
Into the future and not accept failure or settle for less
Than what I'm worth, because my currency is success.

My mistakes are my learning trends,
Living within my means is not a means to an end,
It means that sacrifices now will put me in better stead
To provide for me, my lady, and my children.

Secured I am now, my crooked smile is now genuine,
Even though the world is cold and filled with many differ-
ences.

The difference is that now my mindset is elevated,
And no longer will I focus on the part of me that was
tainted.

74

DAYS OF MY LIFE

God,
Only you know what's my purpose,
Speak to me in this poem,
I'm giving you the focus.

Only you can judge me
So right now I seek repentance
For the wrongs that I have done,
For everything I've put before them.

Them being my family,
Them being my friends,
Them being that someone
Who stood by me since we began.

Them being myself
For I was my own demise,
I smiled for the public –
But in private I've been crying.

I've been trying and Lord, you know,
I've been saying but I have also shown
That when you get a second chance
You need to hold on and not let go.

So if loving me is hard I sincerely apologize,

I've been broken, traumatized.
I've been hurting, I've been tried.
I've been tested,
But each exam I intend to pass,
Though time is of the essence
Like sands through the hourglass.

These are the days of my life,
Trips to Salem I took to express my mind.
And from Genesis to Revelations
My intention will always be to stay true to you and me.

WORTHY

I often ask myself, *"Am I worthy enough?"*
Worthy enough to walk the streets of gold that you cre-
ated?
Worthy enough to be in your presence and call upon
your name?
Am I worthy enough to give you honor even through my
shame?
But I stand here acknowledging that you've kept me on
this path
From the seed planted within my mother to where I am.
Am I worthy enough?
And just when I asked these questions that were weigh-
ing on me,
You told me to wait on you and I shall see that I am
Worthy enough because out of dirt you formed me
Like a potter with clay, you molded me
Into the person I am today
A royal priesthood, a holy nation
You called me by name and I am yours
For I am worthy enough and for that, I give you the honor
and glory
I worship you for you are the ship that sails me through all
seas.
I am living proof of your mercy and your love,
So no longer will I ask if I am worthy enough.

ALREADY WON

In my first bout versus you I was nervous,
The battle was me,
An underweight, and you, a heavyweight champion.
Championing me to feel as though I am a disservice.
I wasn't focused under my surface, felt like I was serving
no purpose,
Taking pounds every round until I was knocked out un-
conscious.
The Referee comes and calls the fight, and I am laying
on the floor,
Oblivious to just how much you affected me.
I neglected my responsibilities to appease your every
change in me
Religiously on bended knee, asking God,
"Why is this me?"
Why can't I be stronger like what others often see in me?
Believe me, my sadness passes through the hourglass like
sand,
Standing in my way keeping me away from things I was
to understand,
Like God's plan,
Like God's hand handing me the light he had,
To show me the path against the wrath that had me
down bad.
It was sad,

That I gained the vision that Wanda gave me so I
couldn't see clear,
Under appreciating the journey it took to be here.
But in order to get where I want to be I have to beware
of my fears,
Wear my heart on my sleeve and leave the tears in the
rear.
For too long I had my life in arrears so this is the repay-
ment,
Like a debt collector, I'm coming to claim everything you
said I wasn't made of,
Because this?
This is my moment!
I'm going after everything you tried to prevent with in-
tent,
Cement my legacy in this concrete jungle that you tor-
ment.
Relentless in the pursuit of my happiness, a will to survive,
Ducking and weaving, back against the rope.
Until I see my chance,
I throw my left and upper cut with my right,
A killer combo to show you my worth and my might.
The Referee counts,
"ONE! ... TWO! ... THREE!
My intensity heightened as you're laid out on the canvas.
Then I hear, "FOUR! ... FIVE! ... SIX!"
My arms are in the air, it's fair to say I'm getting anxious.
"SEVEN! ... EIGHT! ... NINE! ... TEN!"
I did it! I've finally defeated you!
Thank God I made it through this rumble in the jungle

For at that moment I felt like the famous Ali,
Floating like a butterfly, stinging like a bee.

Epilogue

THIS IS I

My name is Chris Enrico St. Hill
Here is my description:
5' 9", slim build, "red" skin.
Worldly justified as an Fuck Boy,
Such a terrible combination, like a new-age sin.

Added with poetic words from deep within,
Thought by some as surface speeches,
But my actions to those said words go out to the ones
that they really are supposed to be reaching.
I'm teaching you about me.

Because I no longer wish to live in fantasies.
The fact is I'm a guy that's trying,
I'm not perfect, but damn it, I'm worth it.
I'm not always good but my bad side isn't far from it.
I hurt just like the next person, have the scars to show you
if you doubt it.

Being a good guy with a good heart doesn't keep a
woman.
I know this to be true,
Because she'll still do you wrong if she feels the urge to.
Don't get it twisted – we as men fail our women at times
too,

In times when we should be down for one, we're out here
trying two.

I'm sorry,
I fell off the handle a bit,
But on that note, I keep saying sorry over and over again.
I mean it when I say it but it's not taken well often,
But I'll keep my hands up and suffer the consequences of
my actions because...

I wasn't supposed to be here
I was left in the sea alone one day to die,
But God said,
"Son?
You're not done!"
So he extended my life,
And now I'm living for his purpose without asking why.

He brought life changers in,
Took life dangers out,
Told me "Love doesn't cost a thing and I'm showing you
the zero-balance account."
Until the next time when I feel like sharing what my life's
about,
I'll move in silence, and let my success be the one to
shout.

This is
Enrico

About The Author

Chris Enrico St.Hill is a Barbadian poet and author.
He believes his art resonates with others by aiding them
with healing as well as inspiring them.
He is very family and goal oriented, passionate, and ro-
mantic.
He is someone who loves hard and believes in the power
of love in its deepest form which will be showcased in
this book

Thank YOU!!!

Thank you for reading my first book This Is I.
Be sure to follow the author on social media at the links
below:

IG: @enricosuave1215
FB: Chris St. Hill
Twitter: @enricosuave2

9 789769 703124